If you love to make jewelry like I do and enjoy learning al[l] latest wire working methods, Down to the Wire is the book for you. You'll learn many new and easy techniques for making wire jewelry and home decor, and find dozens of ideas for using beads with wire. Colored wire, pliers and a few simple tools... that's all you need to create your own unique collection!

Tools

Tools - Knitting needles, cutters, needle nose pliers and round nose pliers.

Pliers are used to remove kinks, straighten bent wire, turn loops and bend straight wire. Pliers are available in many types and sizes. Round nose pliers are invaluable for making spirals, turning loops and bending soft curves. You'll also need a good pair of broad, flat pliers f or holding and stabilizing.

Wire Cutters are used to cut wire from spools, trim ends from finished pieces and any other cutting that needs to be done. Cutters are available at any hardware store. There are cutters built into most general purpose pliers, but they are impractical for trimming close. A nail clipper is handy for this job.

Electric Drill. Make coils quickly and twist spokes for a basket with ease.

Nails are inexpensive and they come in many different shapes and sizes. They can be used to make jigs or to wrap coils for beads and jumprings.

Wood Blocks are used to make jigs. You can also insert a wood block into the base of a basket to help keep the sides straight square.

Easy Wire Techniques

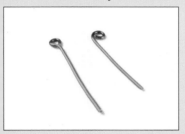

Turning a Loop is one of the most basic techniques. Loops form the basis for spirals, coiled basket bases, links and connectors.

1. Grasp the end of the wire with round nose pliers. Make the loop by turning the pliers away from you. Guide and help form the loop with your thumb.

2. To make an end loop, reposition the jaws of the pliers and bend the base of the loop at a 90° angle to center the loop on the wire.

How to Make Spirals

Spirals. Use them to finish a basket, to form a sturdy base or as decorative jewelry links. They are easy to make.

1. Grasp the loop with flat pliers and turn the wire around the loop, guiding it with your thumb. Reposition the pliers as you work.

2. Eventually the spiral may become large enough to dispense with the pliers. You can simply grasp the coil and turn it, guiding the wire with your thumb.

How to Make Wire Coils

Coiling. Wire coils are used to make jumprings and beads among other decorative items. You can make coils by hand, but using a drill makes it fast and easy.

1. Insert a knitting needle, nail, dowel or pencil into the chuck (where you would normally place a drill bit). Next insert the end of the wrapping wire. Tighten the chuck.

2. Squeeze the trigger of the drill slowly. Guide the wire into a coil with your fingers, making sure the coils are uniform.

Fountain Fun

Water cascades over a rainbow of swirling colored wire on its way to a stone filled basin in this whimsical fountain. You'll love the soothing sound of softly flowing water and the tranquility it adds to any corner of your home.

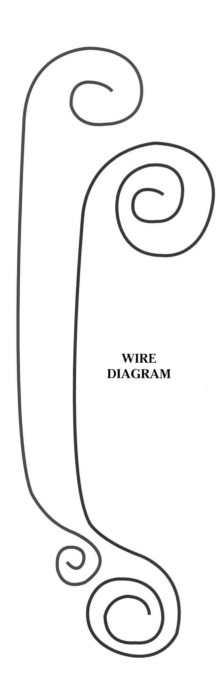

**WIRE
DIAGRAM**

You'll Need
• Fountain pump • 4" Flower pot • 6" Saucer • 16 gauge wire • Pebbles or River stones

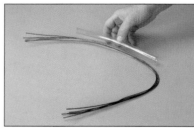

1. Cut the tubing that came with your pump to 8". Cut several 18" lengths of wire and place them along the tubing as shown.

Secure the 18" wires to the top 3" of tubing by wrapping with a tight coil of wire.

2. Bend the bottom wires at a 90° angle and turn into spirals of various sizes. Thread the tubing through the bottom of the flower pot and bend the spirals around it.

3. Trim some of the top wires an inch or so and spiral the ends. Bend the spirals into a tree shape.

4. Connect the pump to the tubing inside the flower pot and place it in the center of the saucer. Fill the space between the pot and the saucer with pebbles. Fill the saucer with water and turn on the pump.

'Float' Glass Fantasies

Wire Wrapped Frames

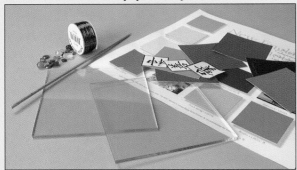

You'll Need
- 2 squares of double strength window pane or 'float' glass
- Paint chips
- 26 gauge wire for wrapping
- Small beads
- Bamboo skewers
- 18 gauge wire for hanger

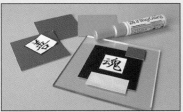

1. Clean and dry glass squares. Use glue stick or double stick tape to secure paint chips and items to be framed to one square of glass.

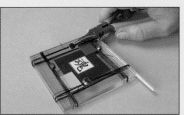

2. Place second piece of glass over design aligning edges. Place skewer along top edge of glass. Cut a length of wire and wrap around one side of glass several times catching skewer in the wraps. Place a bead on one end of wire, slip other end through bead and position on glass. Wrap each end of wire around all wires several times to secure bead. For disk beads, bring both ends of wire up through bead and twist each end around wires.

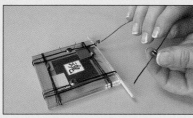

3. Trim ends of skewer 1/2" to 1" longer than glass. Thread 18 gauge hanger wire through 26 gauge wire wraps in front of skewer, make a loop and twist to secure end. Thread 2 disk beads on wire, push against twists. Thread 2 more disk beads and repeat for other end.

Copy these 'Zen' Symbols on a copy machine.

Spirit or Soul

Love

Good or Right

Candle Box

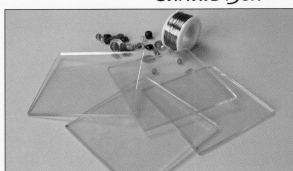

You'll Need
- Four 4" squares of double strength window pane or 'float' glass
- 22 gauge wire for wrapping
- Round nose pliers
- Assorted beads

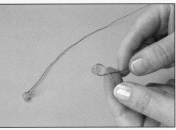

1. Cut 5 feet of wire. Thread bead on end and twist a loop around the bead.

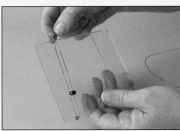

2. Place wire across glass with connecting bead extending beyond end of glass. Thread a bead on the wire, wrap around front of glass, add a bead and wrap around back. Loop wire around end bead.

3. Place connecting bead near edge of glass and twist bead to tighten wire against glass. Wrap remaining wire around glass and twist around last bead.
Tip: Wire will be loose as you wrap. It will be tightened later.

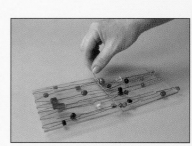

4. To tighten wrapped wire, grab wire with round nose pliers and twist to bend wire and take up slack.
Tip: Stagger the twist placement.

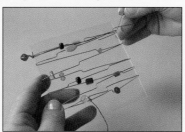

5. Repeat Steps 1 to 4 for remaining 3 sides of box. Cut two 4" pieces of wire. Catch a wire at edge opposite connecting bead and twist end to secure. Repeat for second connecting bead. Add 4" wire pieces to remaining sides of box.

6. To assemble candle box, wrap 4" pieces of wire from one side around the connecting beads of adjacent side. Repeat for remaining 3 corners.

Gourd & Mâché Coiled Baskets

Use a gourd or a paper-mâché box and an easy basket making technique to make these truly unique baskets. Trim them with old coins and beads and fill with treasures. Add a wire dragonfly for a touch of nature…the results are spectacular!

1. Paint gourd or paper mâché box. Punch or drill $1/16$" holes at 1" intervals $1/4$" from top of gourd or box.

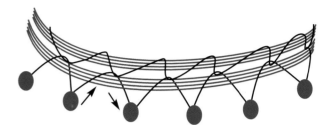

Joining Stitch Diagram

2. Cut enough lengths of 22, 24 and 26 gauge wires to form a $1/4$" thick bundle. Twist plenty of this core wire. You cannot add wire after the basket is started.
For reference, we used 20 feet of core wire for the 4" blue and green box. Place one end of core wire against the side of box. Fold cut end to inside and begin stitching the core to box with 26 gauge wire as shown.

3. Continue stitching the core to the box. Use joining stitches to connect core to the previous row. Placement of the core on the previous row determines the shape of the basket. At the end of the last row, clip core 1" from last joining stitch and fold to inside of basket.

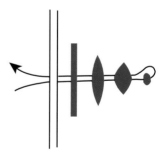

Beading Diagram for Square Box

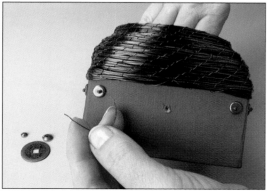

4 . Add beads to holes around top of gourd or drill new holes in box. Cut 36" of 28 gauge wire. Twist a small bead on end of wire. Bring wire through a hole from inside to outside of gourd. Thread a 6mm disk bead, a size 6 seed bead and a size 11 seed bead. Thread wire back through size 6 seed bead, disk bead and back inside basket. Bring wire out through next hole and repeat around basket.
Tip: Coins or found objects may also be used to decorate baskets.

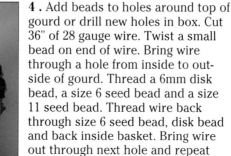

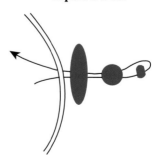

Beading Diagram for Round Box

Note: See directions for making dragonfly on page 12.

Down to the Wire 9

Clay Critter Pins

Fanciful critters made with oven bake clay and wire coils are sure to bring a chuckle to anyone young or old. Make them into pins, pendants or magnets. Or just place a few on desks or shelves to bring a moment of fun to any day.

1. Knead clay until soft. Roll out a ⅛" thick sheet of clay. If using a pasta machine, use setting one. Cut out shapes using template. Cut wires to specified length. Refer to photo to shape wires for legs, antennae, wings, tails, etc.

2. Place one clay body piece on work surface. Place wires on clay. Cover with second clay body piece and press together firmly. Smooth edges.

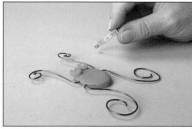

3. Add eyes and trim pieces. Bake. Glue on pin back with Quick Grab.
Tip: Because of the wire inserts, these pieces require a shorter baking time. Check pieces often while baking.

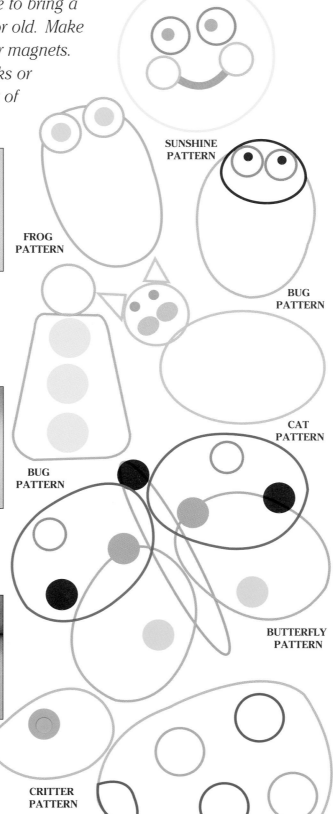

SUNSHINE PATTERN

FROG PATTERN

BUG PATTERN

BUG PATTERN

CAT PATTERN

BUTTERFLY PATTERN

CRITTER PATTERN

You'll Need
- 26 gauge wire
- Rusty tin shapes
- Assorted beads
- Pin backs
- Spray acrylic sealer

1. Spray back of tin shape with several coats of sealer. Let dry. Cut 36" of 22 to 26 gauge wire. Tie knot on one end and thread on several small beads. Hold other end of wire in place on back of metal shape. Randomly wrap wire around shape placing beads as desired.

2. Wrap rusty shape with many layers of different colored wire.

Tip: To add texture, grab random wires and twist with round nose pliers to bend.

Wire Wrapped Pins

Rusty tin
shapes are from
Decorator &
Craft Corp.

Attach pin back with
gauge wire.

Wire Webs

Catch dreams in these gleaming wire webs. This 21st century version of an ancient craft will add beauty to any decor from traditional to ultra modern. These elegant webs make ideal gifts for all ages and genders.

Dream Catcher Box

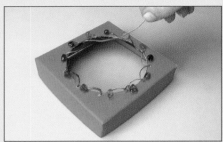

1. Purchase a box with a circle opening on lid or cut out circle. Use a drinking glass to draw circle. Use a colored box or paint a paper mâché box with acrylic paint. Punch an even number of holes ⅛" from edge of opening. Stitch beads in place with 26 gauge wire.

2. Cut three 36" pieces of 26 gauge wire. Use 3 different colors. Holding wires together, tie a knot at one end and push other end up through a hole. Loop wires up through every third hole as shown. When you reach the starting point, begin working in the loops as shown.

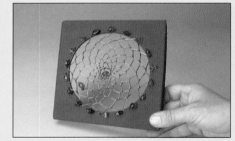

3. To add new wires, push end of old wires through a bead. Push end of new wires into other side of bead. Coil ends of wires at each side of bead to secure.

4. Continue working until the loops become too small to work easily. Start working in every other loop. Do not worry if the work looks uneven, the dream catcher should resemble a spider web. Place a bead in the center and secure with several wraps of wire.

Wire Dream Catcher

Cut six 36" pieces of 16 gauge green and blue wires. Loop wires into a 6" circle leaving about 4" loose at one end and 14" loose at the other end. Cut a 16" piece of 16 gauge tinned copper wire and make a 1½" coil around wires to secure circle. Make web with 2 strands of 26 gauge blue wire. Referring to photo, trim and coil ends of wire.

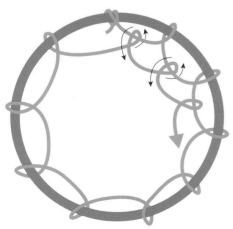

WIRE DREAM CATCHER DIAGRAM

BOX DREAM CATCHER DIAGRAM

Legend of the Dream Catcher

Dream Catchers are made from circles woven with spider web-like patterns.

Place one near the head of a baby or loved one while sleeping. Good dreams float down to bless the sleeping one with trouble-free dreams.

Native American myths of the great plains speak to us of the Dream Catcher. Each woven web will catch Bad Spirit Dreams and hold them until the morning sun evaporates them with the dew.

Good Dreams find their way through the center hole and enter the personal life of the dreamer.

Open Work Baskets

Basket with Open Section

Purchase basket with open section. Weave wire in an over and under pattern until space is filled. Use a single strand of 18 to 20 gauge wire or 3 to 4 strands of smaller wire. Vary colors as desired.

Trim

Add trim details like coiling the handle and replacing the rattan binding with coiled wire. Refer to Rusty Pins on page 12 for instructions on wrapping tin shapes.

Make Open Area

Create your own open area for weaving by removing a woven section from a purchased basket.

Fill open section with woven wire.

Outside Wire Work

BASKET - Add wire work to the outside of a purchased basket. Weave wire over one spoke and under the next spoke. Since most baskets are made with an odd numbers of spokes, the wires will cross on the second row.

HANDLE - Make a criss cross pattern by wrapping the wire one way, then turn to wrap a second way. Wrap around the handle and accessories loosely to finish.

Bud Vases

Dram Bottle Bud Vase

Tip: Dram bottles are used to store essential oils. They may be purchased at container or aromatherapy shops. Test tubes and spice jars may also be used to make bud vases.

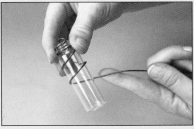

1. Cut 36" of 14 gauge wire. Turn a loop in one end. Place loop at top of bottle and spiral wire around bottle following threads. Then spiral wire down rest of bottle.

2. At bottom of bottle, make 2 tight spirals. These spirals support the weight of the vase. Turn another loop under vase by wrapping wire around an empty dram bottle. Secure loop by wrapping with 22 gauge wire.

3. Cut a piece of wood for the base that will provide adequate support for the vase. Drill a hole in center of base to hold wire. Sand and paint base. Insert wire in base and glue to secure.

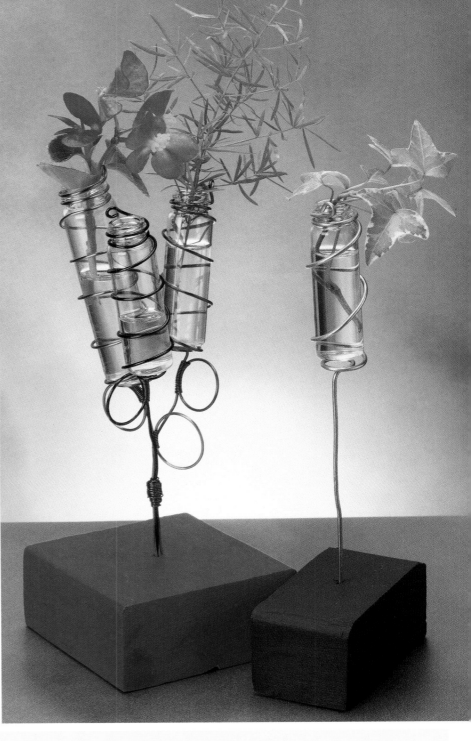

1. Cut 36" of 14 gauge wire. Turn a small spiral in one end. Place thumb over spiral to hold in place on bottle and make several loose wraps around neck of bottle. Leave last 4" straight. Pull out the last few spirals. Starting 1" from end, turn 2 tight spirals and turn a loop in end.

Plant Starter

2. Cut 10" of 16 gauge wire. Turn a loop on each end and bend as shown. Bend wire around a cylinder, such as a roll of pennies or a thick dowel, to help form curves. Wrap the joins with 24 gauge wire.

3. Cut 3" of 16 gauge wire. Turn a loop at one end. Thread on a large hole bead. Trim end and turn a loop.

See Plant Starter photo on page 25.

Wired for Christmas

Need a Christmas tree for a desk or tabletop? These wire and jeweled beauties will shine with a metallic luster throughout the holiday season. Use your assortment of treasured beads to make the trees even more special.

Spiral Tree

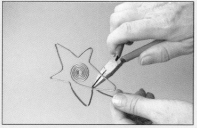

1. Cut 36" of 18 gauge wire. At one end, make a tight ¾" spiral. Then shape rays of star using template. Do not cut wire.

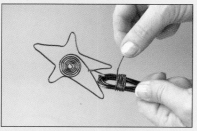

2. Cut eighteen 36" pieces of green and blue 16 gauge wire. Fold each piece in half. Loop stem of star around fold. Then wrap bundle of wires tightly for ½".

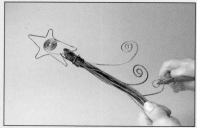

3. Cut 4", 6", 10" and 14" lengths of wire. Coil ends into spirals.

Star Template

Copper Tube Tree

1. Cut 42" of ¼" copper tube. With flat nose pliers, squeeze copper plumber's tube flat. The tube comes in a coil. Do not straighten coil. As you squeeze the tube flat, it will automatically form a tighter coil. With pliers gently squeeze and bend tube into a spiral.

2. Cut 84" of 20 gauge wire. Coil wire tightly around a pencil. Remove from pencil and stretch out to make a long series of loops. Cut 60" of 28 gauge wire. Hold loops along tube and wrap in place with 28 gauge wire.

3. String 42" of size 6 seed beads on 26 gauge wire. Hold strung beads along tube and wrap in place with 28 gauge wire.

4. Cut 2" pieces of 20 gauge wire. Turn a loop on one end, thread on a bead, turn a loop on other end and attach to loops on tree.

5. Make star following instructions for rusty tin shapes on page 12. Wrap excess wire around top of tree to secure.

Make the star any size you like.

Wire Bound Books

1. Make the Book - Each cover is made using 2 pieces of mat board with a space in between for the book to open and close. Glue the mat board to the decorative paper cover leaving a space twice the thickness of the mat board plus 1/16". Trim the corners on the diagonal as shown. Fold and glue the sides.

2. Hinges - Cut pieces of decorative paper and glue them into position as shown.

3. Cut two pieces of decorative paper and glue them to the inside covers.

4. Cut or tear pages slightly smaller than the covers.

5. Clamp the covers with the pages in position on a flat surface. Punch or drill holes for the wire bindings.

Yellow Book

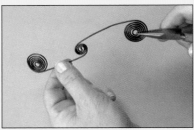

1. Turn front piece beginning at the center of the wire.

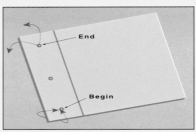

2. Turn a spiral on each end of wire.

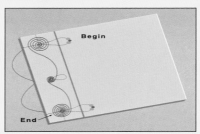

3. Binding Diagram - Use 20 to 24 gauge wire for binding. Turn spirals in ends.

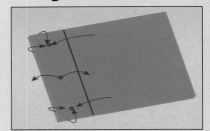

4. Attach front piece with 24 gauge wire. Twist ends of wire on back to secure.

Green Book

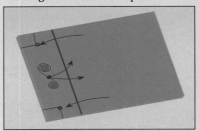

1. Use 20 to 24 gauge wire for binding. Turn ends in spirals.

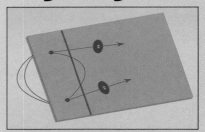

2. Turn ends in spirals.

Brown Book

Use 20 to 24 gauge wire for binding. Turn a spiral in the upper wire and a coil in the lower wire.

BOOKMARKS

Scout.
meeting
Tus. 7:30!

Christmas
Party
December 23

Guess
who?

Gift Wrap & Ties

Name Box

1. Use computer or copy machine to print out name in easy to trace letters. Use a piece of foam core board or a stack of newspaper as a work surface. Cut a piece of heavy-duty aluminum foil larger than name. Cut out name, center on foil and trace over letters with a ball point pen. Trim foil to desired shape. Turn foil over and emboss a line 1/16" from all edges.

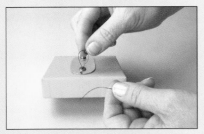

2. Place foil on box lid and punch a hole at each end with a nail. Twist a small bead on one end of 18" piece of 26 gauge wire. Thread up through box lid, foil, disk bead and small glass bead. Go back through disk bead and box lid. Repeat for other side. Twist end of wire to secure.

Spiral Tag Box

1. Cut 18" of 20 gauge wire and mark center. Use your finger to turn a spiral from each end to the center. Cut 3" of 20 gauge wire and form into a spiral. Thread on a teardrop bead and make a loop at end of wire.

2. Cut enough 26 gauge wire to go around box twice plus 4". Fold wire in half and thread one end through center hole in one spiral. Thread on a small glass bead and center bead on doubled wire. Push wire back through spiral. Repeat for second spiral. Wrap wire around box and twist ends together. Cut 3" of 20 gauge wire and attach drop bead spiral to center of double spiral, coil ends.

Flower Tag Box

1. Cut 48" of 22 gauge wire. Wrap around 3/4" wide piece of cardboard. Remove from cardboard. Cut 6" of 26 gauge wire and thread through loop. Twist wire to gather loops into flower shape. Trim ends of wire.

2. Cut 2 pieces of 26 gauge wire long enough to wrap around box twice. Twist a glass bead on one end of wire. Thread other end through center of flower. Wrap wire around box and twist around bead. Trim ends of wire.

A B C D E F G H I J K L M
N O P Q R S T U V W X Y Z
a b c d e f g h i j k l m
n o p q r s t u v w x y z

Votive Hangers

Purple Hanger

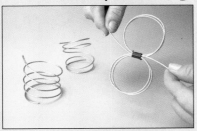

1. Cut 24" of 16 gauge wire. Make 4 loops around a 1¾" mailing tube. Remove coils from tube, hold one side in each hand and open until 2 loops lie flat on each side. Wrap center with 16 gauge wire.

2. Pull each end of wire with pliers so the inner coil on each side becomes smaller. Coil the ends of the wire.

3. Make a votive holder following instructions for Green Holder but use 56" of wire. The extra length is used to make more coils that will be stretched out.

4. Connect pieces and make caged glass piece for bottom.

Green Hanger

1. Cut 40" of 14 gauge wire, find the center and turn a loop on each side of center.

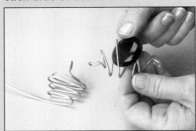

3. To make cage for glass disk, cut 24" of 14 gauge wire. Bend a loop at one end. Turn loop at 90° angle. Make an open, flat spiral. Make a loop on other end. Bend top open, slip glass disk into cage and bend back to close.

2. Trim ends to the same length. Turn a spiral on each end of wire. To finish, wrap center section with coil of 20 gauge wire.

4. Votive Holder - Cut 48" of 14 gauge wire. Loosely coil wire around glass votive cup starting 6" from bottom end of wire. Tightly coil last 6" to support weight of votive cup. Turn center loop down 90° for a hanging loop. Pull out last few spirals at top of holder. Starting 2" from end, turn 2 tight spirals and turn a loop in end.

5. Connect loops and finish bottom with spiral referring to photo.

Red Hanger

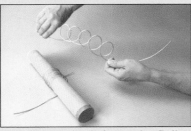

1. Leaving 6" straight on each end, coil wire around a 1¾" mailing tube. Remove coils from tube. Pull and stretch out coils until they look like the photo.

2. Bring wire together just below coils to form a flower shape. Wrap center & bottom sections with 16 gauge wire. Trim ends of 14 gauge piece to 3". Turn a loop in each end.

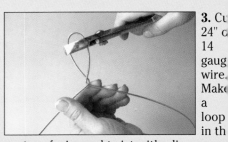

3. Cut 24" of 14 gauge wire. Make a loop in the center of wire and twist with pliers.

4. Turn wire around a pencil 1" from twist. Trim end to desired length, turn a loop.

5. Make the votive holder following instructions for Green Hanger. Finish the top with a spiral as shown in photo.

6. Connect loops and finish the bottom with a spiral referring to the photo.

See Instructions for 'Star' hanger on page 17.

See Instructions for 'Star' hanger on page 17.

Flower Pots

What an ingenious way to decorate your plain terra cotta flowerpots. Add a little paint. Then make wired insects or flowers to hang from the rim. Plants have never looked so good!

Butterfly Flowerpot

1. Paint pot with acrylic paint.

2. Cut 12" of 18 gauge wire and make a 1" coil, trim ends. Cut 10" and 12" pieces of 18 gauge wire. Bring ends together and thread up through coil leaving a 2" loop at bottom. Coil each end into a spiral.

3. Fold 12" piece of wire in half, Thread ends down through coil and bend each end into a spiral.

4. Place butterfly against pot rim and bend loop down to hold in place.

Variations: Larger wings may be on top or bottom of butterfly or the wings can be the same size.

Rusty Metal Shapes Flowerpot

Bend wire hanger following diagram. Wire and bead rusty shapes following instructions on page 12. Attach to hanger and place on pot.

RUSTY METAL SHAPES HANGER DIAGRAM

BUTTERFLY HANGER DIAGRAM (shown from back)

FLOWER DIAGRAM

Flowerpot with Beads

1. For each 1½" flower, drill a hole in pot rim about ¼" from edge. Paint flowerpot.

Tip: Soak flowerpot in water overnight to soften and make drilling easier. Let dry thoroughly before painting.

2. Cut 24" of 20 gauge wire and wrap around 2 pencils to make an oval coil. Fan coil out as shown to make 8 petals. Bend into a circle and clip ends of wire.

3. To attach flower to pot, twist a small bead on the end of a 24" piece of 28 gauge wire. Thread through flower pot from inside to outside. Run wire through center petals, center of a medium to large bead for center of flower and an E bead. Thread wire back through large bead and pot. The pressure of the large bead holds the flower in place.

Wire Baskets with Beads & People

Star Bottom Basket

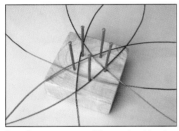

1. Cut 36" pieces of 18 gauge wire. Cut 5 pieces for 5-point star or 6 pieces for 6-point star. To make jig, hammer finishing nails into wood block using pattern. Place the center of each wire between 2 nails. Place the left side of the last wire under the right side of the first wire. See diagram.

4. Cut enough 18 gauge wire to make 3 loops of the required size for rim of basket. Twist ends to hold loops together. Coil ends of basket side wires around rim above last twist.

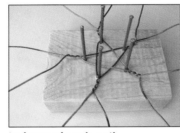

2. Bring the wires on the left and right of each nail together and make 3 twists in front of each nail.

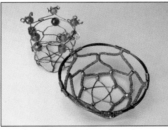

Coiled Bead Basket - Slip coiled wire beads over twists or use beads to join wires instead of twists.

Green Bead Basket - This basket uses metal beads instead of twists. Smaller beads are threaded on the wire. Adding beads to wire produces a more uniform look.

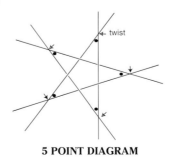

5 POINT DIAGRAM

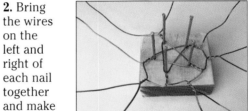

3. Separate pairs of wires and twist alternating pairs together 3 times. Make 6 sets of twists.

Note: To maintain the proper tension and to hold the star in position, keep the work on the jig for the first 2 rows. Experiment while working second row. Twists close to the first row twists produce a tall basket. Twists that lie flat on the jig produce a wide basket.

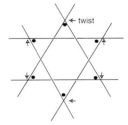

6 POINT DIAGRAM

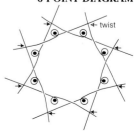

8 POINT DIAGRAM

For anyone who loves baskets, these little jewels are a must. The star bottoms are a visual treat. And best of all, these little baskets are a snap to make using a simple jig. Plain or with a ring of wired friends, you have a work of art.

Friends Baskets

1. Make jig using pattern. Make basket following diagram for star basket n page 28. Trim ends of wire to 8".

2. Make first set of twists on new row and slide a large hole bead over the twists.

3. Shape arms. Add a final twist.

4. Slip a bead over twist for head. Coil, crimp or curl ends of wires form hair.

5. Bend wires below the body to form knees.

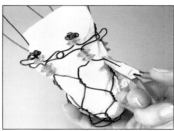

6. Make remaining friends interlocking arms as shown.

Wire Friends

Create a circle of friends to hug a candle. Join hands to wrap a candle..

Legend says that if you give this shaped wire sculpture to a person you care about, the bond of friendship will be cemented forever. Handcrafted, its primitive design is rooted in the custom of gathering around a fire to celebrate peace and brotherhood. Place a candle, a plant or potpourri in the center.

Turn wire into friendship gifts by making tiny people. Make one of them to match every family member. Kids will love to share or trade them with buddies. The results are truly symbols of love.

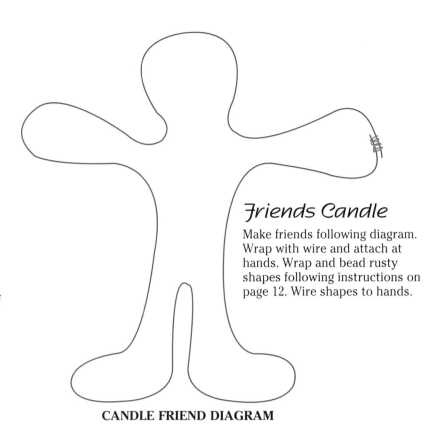

Friends Candle

Make friends following diagram. Wrap with wire and attach at hands. Wrap and bead rusty shapes following instructions on page 12. Wire shapes to hands.

CANDLE FRIEND DIAGRAM

Friends

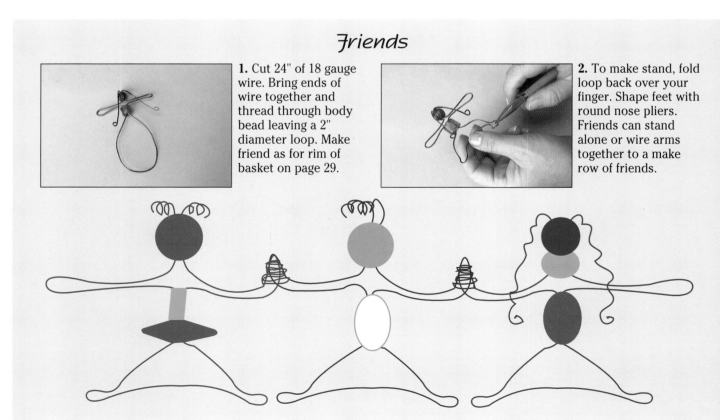

1. Cut 24" of 18 gauge wire. Bring ends of wire together and thread through body bead leaving a 2" diameter loop. Make friend as for rim of basket on page 29.

2. To make stand, fold loop back over your finger. Shape feet with round nose pliers. Friends can stand alone or wire arms together to a make row of friends.

Earring Elegance

These jewel bright earring holders are a colorful way to display your favorite earrings. Use dowels or a simple stretcher frame, a little paint, beads and some imagination…a holder as artistic as the jewels it displays.

Jewelry Holder

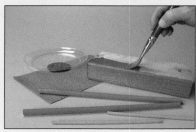

1. Cut 4" x 8" wood base. Drill a ³⁄8" hole centered and ¹⁄2" from each end of base. Cut two 10" pieces of ³⁄8" and two 6¹⁄4" pieces of ³⁄16" dowel. Drill ³⁄16" holes halfway through dowel ¹⁄2" and 3¹⁄2" from end of each ³⁄8" dowel. Drill ⁷⁄16" holes halfway through dowel 1" and 4" from end of each dowel. Sand and paint all wood pieces.

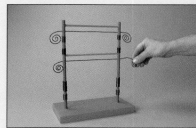

2. Glue small dowels into holes in larger dowels and larger dowel into base. Referring to photo, wrap different colors and gauges of wire around dowels. Cut two 12" pieces of 16 gauge wire, insert into larger dowels and bend each end into a spiral.

Jewelry Tree

You'll Need
- Wood block
- 16 gauge wire
- ³⁄8" and ³⁄16" dowels
- Drill
- ³⁄8", ³⁄16" and ¹⁄16" drill bits
- White or wood glue
- Foam brush

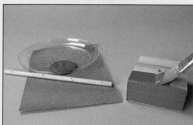

1. Sand wood block. Drill ³⁄8" hole in center of block. Cut 12" piece of ³⁄8" dowel. Drill four ¹⁄16" holes in dowel spaced about 2" apart.

2. Cut 6", 8", 12" and 18" pieces of wire graduating sizes from smallest at top to largest at bottom. Using photo as a guide, turn a spiral in each end with round nose pliers. Have fun shaping spirals keeping in mind the length and size of your earrings.

3. Secure spirals to dowel by wrapping with 16 gauge or smaller wire. Glue dowel into hole in base.

Hardware Cloth Jewelry Holder

You'll Need
- 8" x 10" stretcher frame
- 6¹⁄2" x 8¹⁄2" piece of hardware cloth
- 20 gauge copper wire
- Assorted glass beads
- Acrylic paint
- Round nose pliers.

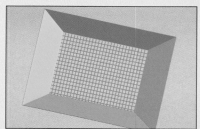

1. Assemble and paint stretcher frame. Center hardware cloth behind frame.

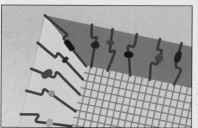

2. Wrap a loop around each corner, 7 loops on short sides and 9 loops on long sides, bring wire loosely around frame and threading through hardware cloth. Add a bead on each loop. Secure ends on back and cut off excess wire. With pliers, make bends in loops as shown.

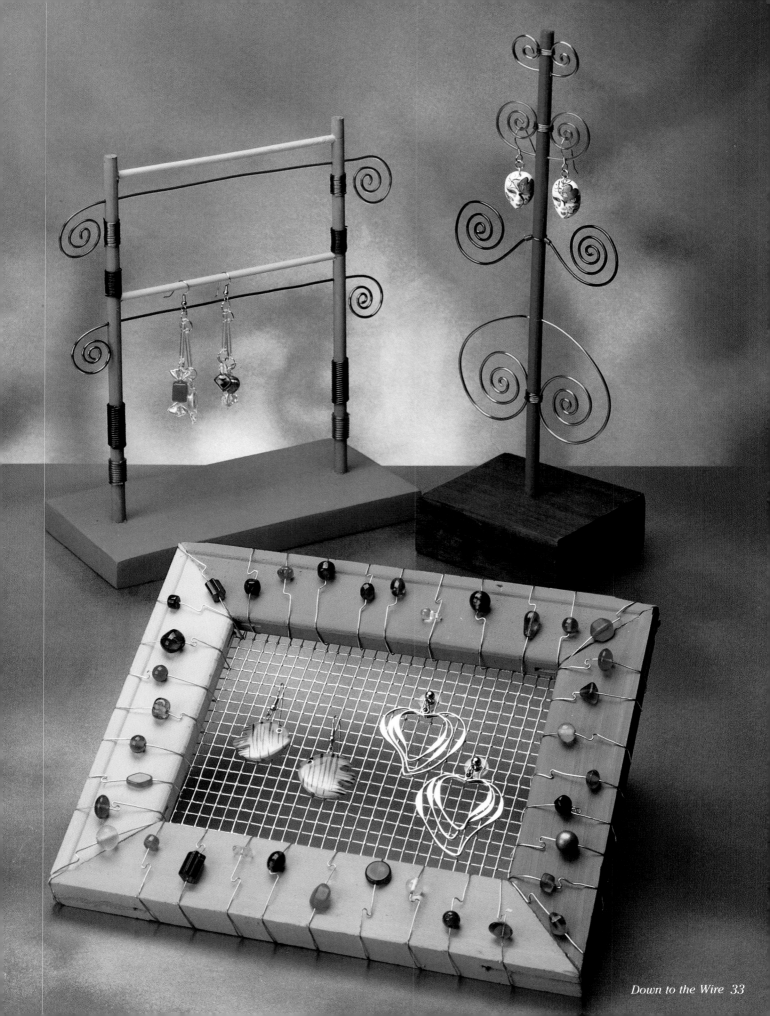